STEP-UP Books

are written especially for children who have outgrown beginning readers. In this exciting series:

- the words are harder (but not too hard)
- there's more text (but it's still in big print)
- there are plenty of illustrations (but the books aren't picture books)
- the subject matter has been carefully chosen to appeal to young readers who want to find out about the world around them. They'll love these informative and lively books.

KIDS DO AMAZING THINGS

Imagine
- dancing on top of a hot-air balloon
- doing 25,222 sit-ups in a row
- performing on a trapeze in a world-famous circus

Kids have done all these things—and a lot more too! From Betty Bennett, who flew an airplane by herself when she was only 10, to Bobby Fischer, a chess whiz at age 12, here are nine stories of truly amazing boys and girls.

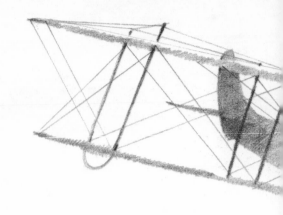

KIDS Do

by Arthur Myers

illustrated by Anthony Rao

Amazing Things

Step-Up Books   Random House
New York

To Tarin Ashley Patrick—one amazing kid

Grateful acknowledgment is made to Jobete Music Company, Inc., for use of lyrics from "Baby Love," Copyright © 1964 by Jobete Music Company, Inc., and for use of lyrics from "Stop! In the Name of Love," Copyright © 1965 by Jobete Music Company, Inc.

Library of Congress Cataloging in Publication Data:
Myers, Arthur. Kids do amazing things. (Step-up books; no. 30) SUMMARY: Nine brief biographies of 12 youngsters who have achieved renown for unusual accomplishments. Included are an 8-year-old boy who set a new sit-up record, a 10-year-old girl who was the youngest person to fly an airplane solo, and a 12-year-old boy who worked as a stunt kid in the movies. 1. Children—United States—Biography—Juvenile literature. 2. Success—Juvenile literature. [1. Occupations. 2. Biography] I. Title. HQ792.U5M96 301.43'14'0922 [B] [920] 79-20363 ISBN: 0-394-84271-5 ISBN: 0-394-94271-X (lib. bdg.)

Manufactured in the United States of America   1 2 3 4 5 6 7 8 9 0

Contents

King of the Sit-Ups

Richard Knecht (kuh-NECKT) is the youngest and smallest in his family. Maybe that is why he wanted to be best in the world at something.

For many years Richard and his brother and father were acrobats. They called themselves the Balancing Knechts. They used to climb on top of each other and balance. Sometimes they balanced on one hand. Sometimes they balanced on chairs and tables.

The Knechts started the act when Richard was only five. They traveled around the United States. They gave shows at fairs, in theaters, and at shopping centers. They talked to children in schools about keeping healthy and fit.

And in between it all they did exercises. The balancing act put a strain on their bodies. They had to work hard to keep in good shape. Richard became VERY good at doing an exercise called a sit-up.

Richard started doing sit-ups when he was only a baby. He was still in his crib. He would lie down flat. Then he would sit up without moving his legs. This is harder to do than it seems. It takes very strong stomach muscles.

Richard's father would help him. Mr. Knecht would put his hand behind the baby's head. Then Mr. Knecht would smile, and say, "Do a sit-up." And with a little help, Richard would do one.

By the time Richard was eight, he was a sit-up expert. He decided to try for a new world record. Someone had just set a record of about 17,000 sit-ups in a row. Richard would have to do even more.

The Knechts were doing shows in Idaho at the time. Idaho Falls High School let Richard use its gym.

The date was December 23, 1972. More than 500 people came to watch Richard. Three men kept track of the sit-ups. They marked the number on a blackboard.

There were some special rules. Nothing could hold Richard's feet down. But his feet could not leave the floor when he sat up. If they did, the sit-up did not count. Also, Richard was not allowed to bend his knees. These things made the sit-ups very hard.

The crowd cheered as Richard began. Up and down he went. Every couple of hours someone gave Richard a sip of orange juice. But Richard did not stop his sit-ups. Sometimes a high-protein pill was popped into his mouth. Sometimes he was fed a spoonful of honey. Still he did not stop. He kept on doing more than 2,200 sit-ups each hour.

The room was kept at 58 degrees Fahrenheit (15 degrees Celsius). If it were too hot, Richard would sweat. He would become tired. He would have to stop before very long. If the room were too cool, his muscles would tighten up. They would hurt. And that would be the end of his try.

On Richard went, hour after hour. After

about 7 hours, he was close to the old record
of 17,000. Richard kept going, up and
down. Then he passed 17,000! The crowd
gave a yell. A new world record had been
set.

But Richard still felt strong, and he kept
on. He was aiming for 25,000 sit-ups now.
No one had ever even come near doing that
many. After a while, he passed the 25,000
mark!

He began to slow himself down.
He could not stop all of a sudden.
That would make him sick. But
he had done enough. He had set
a great new record.

When he was finished, he had
done 25,222 sit-ups. It took him
11 hours and 14 minutes. The
audience stood and clapped as
though it would never stop.

The Knecht family was very
proud. Richard was the champion
of the world at sit-ups. He was
only eight. Yet he had beaten
records set by grown men.

Richard was so happy
he did a handstand—
on his father's shoulders!

Flying All Alone

Betty Bennett sat in the airplane—all
alone. Her father and brother stood nearby,
watching. They were at a little airfield in
Cuba. Just past the field, Betty could see the
ocean. It was bright and shining in the sun.
She was going to fly the plane by herself. No
one else would be in it with her. This is
called a solo. It would be her first. If she did
it safely, people all over the world would hear
of it. Hundreds of newspapers and magazines
would tell the story of Betty Bennett.
For she was only ten. She would be the
youngest person ever to fly an airplane alone.

Flying in an airplane was not new to Betty or her brother. Their father sold airplanes. And he took the children on many flights. Flying was like riding in a car for the Bennett family. They even had an airfield behind their house in Pennsylvania (pen-sull-VAY-nee-uh). They took off in their plane from the airfield and landed there, too. They parked the plane next to their house the way other families park cars.

Betty began steering planes when she was only four. Of course, her father sat beside her. Al, Jr., also flew. He was two years older than Betty. When he was 11, he made

his first solo. He was the youngest person
ever to do that. Betty wanted to solo, too.
She asked her father to help her.

For a year her father had her drive a car
around the airfield. He wanted her to learn
to handle a machine that was moving. Later
he put her in a plane. She did not fly it. She
just speeded up the engine. And the plane
rolled across the ground. She practiced
steering.

Betty was so small that she had to sit on pillows. These made her high enough to see out the window. Pillows were behind her back, too. They helped her feet reach the floor pedals.

After a few months, Betty began to fly the plane. Her father sat beside her, giving advice. Almost every morning they practiced. Even if the wind was strong, they flew. If the air was rough, they went up anyway. It was all good training for Betty.

In the United States, a person must be 16 to fly alone. Because of this rule, Al, Jr., made his solo flight in Mexico. When Betty was ready to solo, the family flew to Cuba. Betty had been getting ready for almost two years. The year was 1952.

Now she waited for the engine to warm up. She heard her father call, "It's all

yours." She gave the engine more gas. The
plane began to roll. It raced faster and faster
over the grass runway. It lifted into the air!

Betty felt very free and happy. She loved
swooping through the air, free of the
ground. She felt so good she began to sing
"Whistle While You Work." Singing also
kept her from feeling scared.

Betty flew out over the blue, sparkling sea. She made a big circle and came back over the land.

Now she had to come down. This was the hardest part. She had to know just when to slow down the engine. She had to think about which way the wind was blowing. She had to think of the speed of the wind.

The plane began to drop slowly. The ground came up, closer and closer. She felt like a leaf drifting to the ground.

Betty made a perfect landing. Her father rushed over and hugged her. She was the youngest person in the world ever to solo an airplane. Even today, many years afterward, no one younger has done it.

The Boy Who Wouldn't Act Blind

Nine-year-old Sam Lentine (len-TEEN) could ride a bicycle. He rode with other children all around his neighborhood.

He played baseball and softball, mostly center field. Sometimes he pitched. He was only fair at catching the ball. But he was a good hitter.

Sam had a dartboard in his game room. He was good at throwing darts and hitting the target.

What is so strange about all of that? The amazing thing is that Sam was blind.

He was only a year old when he lost his sight. But he was lucky in a way. Sam was psychic (SY-kick). This means he could sense things around him without seeing them. He did not have to touch the things, either. Pictures of them came into his mind in some other way.

Sam could tell where a parked car was standing. He could steer his bike around it. He could sense a tree or a building across a street. So he rarely walked into things. He knew when a ball was coming toward him. Much of the time, he could catch it.

Sam could move his hand above a sheet of paper and tell its color. He could hold his hand above a ball or a shoe and know its shape.

The psychic sense is a strange sense. Probably everyone has it. But few people use it. A blind person needs this sense more than others do. So some blind people use it a great deal. Sam is one of them.

Sam had something else that was special. He had parents who did not treat him like a blind boy. They treated him like his brother, who could see. So Sam acted like any other boy.

In 1948, Sam started going to a school for the blind. He was lively and popular in school. He was also very smart. He quickly became a school leader.

When he was 11, he started a dance band. All its members were blind. Everyone thought they sounded great. Sam played the piano, the bass clarinet, and the saxophone. He also took lessons in tap-dancing.

He became a wrestler, too. Often Sam wrestled with boys who could see. He would pretend he did not know where they were. He knew, all right! His psychic sense told him.

"Then I'd grab them!" Sam laughs.

Sam went on to college. Later he taught in a high school. But Sam wanted to know more about the psychic sense. He wanted to know how it could be used to help people. So he went back to school.

He also started a company called Ability Aids. It teaches handicapped people to help themselves. Many of these people are blind. Sam teaches them how to sense colors and shapes, as he does.

Another thing Sam can do is sense a special glow called an aura (OR-uh). Everyone and everything gives off this glow. But few people can see it. Sam senses the glow through his forehead. He knows the color of a person's aura. From it, he can tell if someone is healthy or sick. He often helps doctors find out what is wrong with their patients.

Being psychic is important to Sam. But more important is the way he was brought up. Most handicapped people are treated as though they are different from others. Sam thinks this is bad. He says, "People will act the way they are expected to act."

Sam was treated like anyone else. He has always tried to live that way.

Circus Family

Clowns, elephants, lion tamers! The Farias (fah-REE-ahss) children see these every day. How did they get so lucky? They are part of the biggest circus in the world. It is called the Ringling Brothers, and Barnum & Bailey Circus.

Julio (WHO-lee-oh), Carmelia, and Tata Farias were born into the circus. Their father and mother did tricks on a trapeze. And now the children do, too. A trapeze is a bar that hangs from two ropes. It is like a swing that is high up in the air.

The Farias children perform with their father. They "fly" from one trapeze to another. They call their act The Flying Farias. Mrs. Farias used to be in the act, too. But she fell from a trapeze. She broke her arm. She does not fly anymore.

Julio is the greatest young trapeze flyer in the world. He started flying when he was only seven. Before that, he practiced on low bars and swings. These are safely close to the ground. When he was ten, Julio learned how to do a triple somersault (SUM-ur-salt). He

lets go of the trapeze and turns over in the air three times. Then his father catches him. He is the youngest person ever to do this trick.

Julio was born in Cuba. So were Mr. and Mrs. Farias. Carmelia and Tata were born in the United States. But they all have seen thousands of miles of America. They travel around in their own house trailer. They follow the circus wherever it goes.

Every few days the Fariases wake up in a new town. They hear the elephants trumpeting, the lions roaring. They smell the sawdust. They see the big tent going up. They are in a show every afternoon and evening. On Saturdays they are in a morning show, too.

The Farias children get their lessons by mail from a school in Baltimore. They study all morning. Their teachers are mostly clowns. There are 30 clowns in this big circus. Most of them are young and have been to college. So they are good teachers.

In the afternoon, thousands of people start coming through the circus gates. The smells of peanuts and cotton candy fill the air. The men called barkers begin shouting in front of the side shows. Show time is near. Everyone is excited.

The Fariases change from their plain slacks and T-shirts. They put on shiny show clothes. Their costumes sparkle in the light.

They hear the clown music. They know the clowns are on, and The Flying Farias are next. They stand near the performers' entrance. Circus people call it the "back door." The band plays their music. They dash to the center of the ring. People cheer. The Fariases smile and bow.

Now the Fariases race up the ladders.
They stand on little platforms high in the
air, and bow again. There is a net below
them. But they can still be hurt if they fall.
Julio once fell and broke his arm in the net.
Another time his head hit his father's jaw
and broke it.

Mr. Farias wraps his legs around a trapeze
bar. He starts swinging, his head down.
Julio swings from another trapeze. Then he
lets go. He sails through the air, his legs stiff.
His father catches him by the hands.

Now it is Carmelia's turn. She does the
same trick. Then little Tata does it, too.

The tricks get harder and harder.
Carmelia does a somersault. She pulls her
knees to her chest and turns over in the air.
She can do a double somersault, too.

Julio, Carmelia, and Tata fly back and forth. Their father is always there to catch them. But a day could come when he might miss. They try not to think of that.

The act ends with Julio's triple somersault. Everyone is quiet. The drums roll. Then he flies, turning, turning, turning through the air! His father catches him. The band plays loudly. And the crowd cheers. The Fariases bow, high on their platforms. They climb down the ladders. They are safe this time!

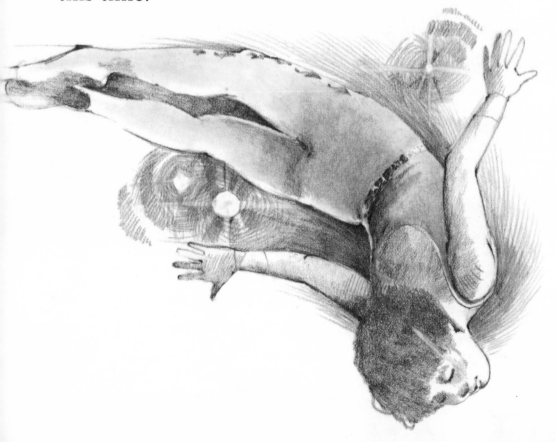

Crazy About Singing

When she was only nine, Stephanie Mills was singing in a Broadway show. A few years later, she was the star of a big Broadway hit called "The Wiz."

How did Steffie get so far so fast? She was special from the time she was a very little girl. Steffie was singing almost before she could talk. At age three, she learned songs from the radio. Instead of talking, she sang to people.

Steffie liked to play with her big brother. If he was reading, she would sing a song popular in 1960, "Stop, stop in the name of love. . . . "

Once Steffie's mother said to a neighbor, "I think Steffie really loves me." Steffie started singing another popular song, "Baby love, baby love . . . "

As Steffie grew older, she liked to imagine

she was a movie director. She would take a mop with long strings. She would pretend it was a woman. A broom would be a man. Steffie would stand them together and pretend they were actors.

She set up chairs. They were her pretend orchestra (OR-kess-truh). Steffie would stand on a box and wave a stick. She was the orchestra leader.

In the summer, she would sit outside her house in Brooklyn and sing. Other little girls would join in. They liked to pretend they were famous.

Steffie had a beautiful voice, and she loved music. Hearing her made people feel good.

When Steffie was nine, her brother saw a newspaper ad. A new show was starting on Broadway. That is where the big shows are put on in New York. The show was called "Maggie Flynn." It was about black children. Her brother took her to the theater. And she tried out. She got a part in the show. She had lines to speak. She had a song all to herself.

Soon Steffie's parents sent her to a school for children who want to act. Her older sister was an actress. She took Steffie with her to places where actors practice.

Then the Apollo Theater in Harlem had an amateur (AM-uh-choor) hour. Amateurs are people who have never been paid to sing or act. Steffie was not really an amateur. She had already been paid for singing. But they let her enter the contest anyway. She won six weeks in a row. Then the theater paid her to sing there for a full week. Soon she made a record for a big company.

Next came her biggest break. She heard about a new show. It was going to be like "The Wizard of Oz." Only all the actors would be black. The show would be full of music. Its name would be "The Wiz."

People told Steffie to try for the leading part, Dorothy. But Steffie was afraid to try. In the show, Dorothy is a little girl. Steffie was already 13. But she was very small. She looked younger than her age. Still, she did not think she would get the part.

The director of the show heard about Steffie. He wanted to see her. She agreed to try out. Three times Steffie sang for the people who were putting on the show. Then, one great day, they told her, "The part is yours."

She played Dorothy for four years. And a dream came true. Steffie became famous.

Steffie expects to sing all her life. To her, singing is like breathing.

She says, "Imagine a world without anyone singing!"

Stephanie Mills surely can't.

The Stunt Kid

The Little League baseball team was throwing the ball around. Nearby, a boy climbed onto a motorcycle. VAROOM, VAROOM, it went. Then the machine took off. The team suddenly stopped. The boy was racing the motorcycle around the bases!

The players jumped out of the way. The man who was coach began screaming. He ran after the boy on the motorcycle.

The boy headed his

motorcycle into the outfield. He turned to
look back at the man chasing him. He didn't
see the outfield fence ahead of him. He crashed
into it, and was thrown off. The motorcycle
fell on its side, wheels spinning.

"Cut!" cried someone. It was a movie
director. He was ordering the cameras to
stop. For this was a movie, "The Bad News
Bears." The coach and the children playing
ball were actors. But the boy on the
motorcycle was not an actor. He was what
movie people call a "stunt kid."

His name is Reid Rondell. At that time he was 12. He had already been a stunt kid for two years.

Reid is part of a movie family. His grandfather was a movie director. His father, Ron, is a stunt man. So is his older brother, Ron, Jr.

Stunt people do things that are too dangerous for actors to do. They fall from high places. They crash cars and bikes into things. They fall off horses. On the screen, it looks as though the actors did the stunts.

Reid had a lot of training before he did "The Bad News Bears" stunt. He had been driving a motorcycle since he was four years old. His father used to take him out in the desert to practice. But motorcycle training alone did not make Reid a stunt person. He had to prepare his body, too.

"You have to be strong," Reid says. "If you land on your shoulder, those muscles must be strong."

Reid began his stunt training when he was about nine. He practiced tumbling. He did weight lifting. He did push-ups and sit-ups. He worked on trampolines with older stunt men. Surfing and water-skiing helped Reid get ready, too.

Reid got his chance to become a stunt person sooner than he expected. One day he went to a TV stage set with his father and brother. The show "Mod Squad" was being taped. Ron, Jr., was going to do his first stunt. But Ron, Jr., was 15. The director thought he was too big. The boy actor was much younger and smaller than Ron. Then the director saw Reid, who was only ten. He asked Mr. Rondell if Reid could do the stunt. And that is how Reid began.

Reid says it was an easy stunt. It was a good way to start. He was not even nervous. The scene was of a man chasing a boy. Reid had to jump in and out of boats. Then he was tackled to the ground. Reid and the stunt man practiced the tackle. They did it slowly at first, without touching. When the scene was shot, they knew just what to do.

"Everything is worked out before we do the stunt," Reid says. "We try to make everything as safe as we can."

Reid was now a real stunt kid. Before long he did a fall on the TV show "Mannix." He practiced by falling into a big bag full of air. When the cameras were rolling, Reid fell about 15 feet (more than 5 meters). "I landed on some cardboard boxes," he says. "The boxes broke my fall."

Reid had to look like a black boy for that stunt. He wore an Afro wig and black make-up.

One of Reid's favorite jobs was being in the movie "Hooper." It was about stunt people. Reid played himself, the world's youngest stunt person. He did a 30-foot fall.

Reid has done a little acting in movies. But he does not want to be an actor. "I want to be a stunt man," he says. "That's it. I always wanted to follow in my father's footsteps. And my mother backs me up one hundred percent."

The Greatest Chess Player
in the World

The boy who walked into the Manhattan Chess Club was only 12. He was nervous. This was the first time he had ever been there. But he was already a good chess player. He had been playing since he was six. He was sure he could beat anyone in the room.

The Manhattan Chess Club is the most important chess club in America. Some of the world's best players belong to it.

A few games of "lightning" chess were going on that day. In most chess games, the players take a long time between moves. They think and think and think. Sometimes they take hours! But in a lightning game, each player has to move within 10 seconds.

The boy had played lightning chess before. So he started a game. Soon everyone in the room had stopped playing. They crowded around the boy. They watched him

make his moves. These were men and
women who had played chess all their lives.
They were amazed at how good this
12-year-old was.

That day in 1956 was the beginning of
fame for Bobby Fischer. Two years later, he
was chess champion of the United States.
He was only 14. At 15 he was a world
champion, or Grand Master. He was called
the greatest player in the history of the
game.

What made Bobby so outstanding at
chess? He was smart, of course. But more
than that, he was a fighter. He wanted to be
the best at whatever he did.

Bobby's sister, Joan, got him started at
chess. She liked to buy him puzzles and
games. One day she bought him a chess
game. She showed him how to play.

Chess is played by two people on a flat board. The board has squares, just like a checker board. But chess is much harder than checkers. Each chess player starts the game with 16 men on the board. Not all the men look the same. There are different rules for the different pieces. Some men can be moved forward only. Others can also be moved backward, or sideways, or at an angle. The game takes a lot of thought and planning. Some of the smartest people in the world play chess.

Bobby was eight when he joined his first chess club. He began to play against very good grown-up players. Sometimes he cried when he lost. But he always came back for another game. Before long he would beat the person who had beaten him.

Most children read comic books for fun.

Bobby read books about chess. He studied
them hour after hour. His mother thought
he was spending too much time on chess.
She tried to get him to stop. She couldn't.
Often he would be out late at night, playing
chess. His mother had to go out looking
for him.

Once he and another player sat in a park through a heavy rainstorm. They would not stop their game until somebody won.

Bobby was not easy to get along with. He called anyone who did not play chess a "weakie." Anyone who did not play as well as he did was a "weakie," too. That made just about everyone in the world a "weakie"—at least in Bobby's mind.

Some people called him rude. Others said they didn't care if he was. They thought he was wonderful anyway. Many people still think Bobby Fischer is the greatest Grand Master there ever was.

Millie the Wing-Walker

Back in the 1910s and 1920s, flying was new. Airplanes had been invented only a few years before. It seemed a wonderful thing that they flew at all.

The new flying machines were like toys to some people. Pilots did all kinds of stunts with their planes. The most daring pilots did fancy turns. They flew upside down. They dived for the ground. But they leveled out just in time. Crowds watched and cheered.

Soon stunt people began to do tricks in the air. They walked on top of airplane wings. They hung from the wheels of the planes. They made parachute (PARA-uh-shoot) jumps for fun.

The youngest of these stunt people was a girl of only ten. Her name was Millie Unger.

Millie's father made and flew giant balloons. He rented some to movie studios. These balloons appeared in films. Mr. Unger put ads on the sides of other balloons. Companies paid him to fly the balloons where people could see them.

Millie was a lively little girl. She had seen movie stunt men walk on balloons. Why couldn't SHE do that, she wondered. Her father thought it was a good idea. He would have someone take moving pictures of Millie on top of the balloon.

The balloon Millie was going to ride was
a hot-air balloon. Hot air is lighter than cool
air. So it rises. If a balloon is filled with hot
air, it will rise.

The balloon was made of silk. It had an
asbestos (as-BESS-tuss) lining. The lining
kept the balloon from burning when the air
was heated.

Mr. Unger set up a stove on a street
corner in Los Angeles. The stove burned
wood. Mr. Unger and his helpers held the
balloon over the hot stove.

Soon the balloon started to rise. Only a thick rope kept it from floating away.

Mr. Unger put a ladder against the balloon. Millie climbed it. She stood on top of the balloon. The top was wide and flat. A man cut the rope. Up, up went the balloon. It floated 1,000 feet (300 meters) above the ground. It went where the wind took it.

Then Millie began to dance. She did a dance of the 1920s called the shimmy. This was in 1925. She waved and yelled to the people on the ground below.

An airplane circled the balloon. In it was a cameraman, taking movies. The film was sold to a movie news company. People

saw it in movie theaters. It is still
shown sometimes on TV.

How did Millie's balloon get down? The
air in it started to cool. The balloon slowly
sank to the ground.

Millie never again went up on top of a balloon. The Los Angeles police would not let her. They thought it was too dangerous. So Millie did wing-walking on airplanes instead!

In those early days of flying, airplanes had no roofs. The seats of planes were open to the wind. A person could climb out. When the plane was in the air, Millie would get out of her seat. She walked out onto the wing. The wind blew at her at 70 miles an hour (112 kilometers an hour). She was never blown off, though.

Sometimes she held on to a leather strap

on the wing. Once a cameraman took movies of her dancing on the wing. The dance was called the Charleston.

But flying was growing older. In 1927 the government made new rules about wing-walking. No one could wing-walk without wearing a parachute. A strong metal post had to be put on the wing. The walker had to be strapped to this post. These rules made wing-walking much safer. But it was not so much fun. Now it seemed too easy. It was not dangerous enough for the daring wing-walkers. They said that now they could not fall off if they tried. And crowds didn't want to watch somebody holding on to a post. Wing-walking died out.

Millie stopped wing-walking. Later in her life she worked as a movie extra. It was not so glorious. But it WAS a lot safer.

The Bionic Boy

Jeff Smith had a favorite television program. It was called "Lost in Space." The character he liked best was not a person. It was a robot. I sure would like to build my own robot, Jeff thought.

Jeff comes from a family that builds things. Both his parents make radios. His two older brothers won prizes in school science fairs. So it was not strange that Jeff would think of making a robot.

For his ninth birthday, he got a set of Tinkertoys. These are long wooden sticks that can be joined. Children use them to build things.

Jeff decided to make his robot from the Tinkertoy sticks. But he would not build a whole robot at first. He would start with one

part. He would make an arm. It would be an arm that really worked. Jeff studied carefully how a real human arm works. Then he set to work.

He used Tinkertoy sticks as the bones of the arm. For power he used a small motor. It ran on batteries. He put the motor where the elbow would be. Then he attached the arm to a tailor dummy. He ran wires from the Tinkertoy arm to his own arm.

Jeff worked on the arm for eight months. He wanted it to move when his own arm moved.

At last Jeff made his final test. Slowly, he moved his own arm. Yes, his invention worked! The dummy's arm moved, too. Now Jeff moved his fingers. The dummy's fingers moved. Jeff picked up a Ping-Pong ball. The dummy's fingers moved to pick one up, too. Jeff was happy.

He named his dummy "Herbie." Herbie was not quite a robot. But he had a robot's arm—a bionic arm. Bionics is the study of how the human body works. Scientists are using what they know to make machines. These bionic machines work just like parts of the human body.

After building Herbie, Jeff made other

bionic arms. Each one was better than the one he built before. One of these arms has metal "bones." It has a wooden "elbow." Jeff put a glove over the bones of the first hand. The newer hands have light balsa wood over the bones. Jeff shaped the wood to look like real hands.

Jeff's newer arms could do almost anything he wanted them to. They could wiggle their fingers. They could pick up small things.

Jeff entered his second bionic arm in a science fair in Indiana. That is where he lives. He won nine prizes. He was sent to a big fair in Denver, Colorado. There were 436 boys and girls in that fair. Jeff was one of six winners. His prize was a week's trip to Washington. Many newspapers and magazines had stories about Jeff.

Now Jeff is working on making that robot.
He wants to build the whole body. So far,
he has made both arms and the lower legs.

"When you get to the part between the
knees and the shoulders, it gets kind of
hard," Jeff says.

But one of these days, he will probably
have a robot walking around.

ABOUT THE AUTHOR

Arthur Myers has spent many years as a newspaper man, magazine editor, writer, and teacher of writing. Recently he has been concentrating on creating books especially for young readers. So far he has had a half-dozen published. *Kids Do Amazing Things* is the first juvenile book he has written for Random House. Mr. Myers was born and raised in Buffalo, New York. For the past 22 years, he has made his home in the Berkshire Hills of western Massachusetts.

ABOUT THE ILLUSTRATOR

Anthony Rao gave up a budding career as an actor to devote all his time to illustrating children's books. After graduating from the Rhode Island School of Design, Mr. Rao became a staff artist for *Highlights for Children* magazine in Pennsylvania. The call of the theater brought him back to the New York City area, where he was born and raised. Although Mr. Rao now spends most of his time drawing dinosaurs and amazing kids—instead of acting—he still lives in New York City.